T0154229

the EMILY VALENTINE *poems*

the EMILY VALENTINE poems

ZOE WHITTALL

Invisible Publishing
Halifax & Picton

Text copyright © Zoe Whittall, 2006, 2016

Library and Archives Canada Cataloguing in Publication

Whittall, Zoe, author
    The Emily Valentine poems / Zoe Whittall. -- Tenth anniversary edition.

Issued in print and electronic formats.
ISBN 978-1-926743-87-5 (paperback).--ISBN 978-1-926743-88-2 (html)

    I. Title.

PS8595.H4975E45 2016   C811'.6   C2016-905496-9
                                           C2016-905497-7

Cover and interior design by Megan Fildes | Typeset in Laurentian
With thanks to type designer Rod McDonald

Printed and bound in Canada

Invisible Publishing | Halifax & Picton
www.invisiblepublishing.com

We acknowledge the support of the Canada Council for the Arts which last year invested $20.1 million in writing and publishing throughout Canada.

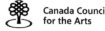

Canada Council   Conseil des Arts
for the Arts   du Canada

For Suzy Q. Malik

INTRODUCTION TO THE TENTH ANNIVERSARY EDITION

Thoughts I had while re-reading this book:

1. Wow, a lot can change in ten years.

2. It's so fun being young and confident for absolutely no reason!

3. Huh, some of these poems are really good.

4. Huh, some of these poems could use another 17 edits.

5. Confident!

6. Wow, so I wrote about that, huh?

7. Prosody! Sometimes.

8. I wrote that line? I have no memory of that.

9. Remember when a blurb from Eileen Myles came in to your inbox (Hotmail?!) and you freaked out with joy? That was a good day.

10. I used to understand line breaks more than I do now. Thank god I did that MFA after I published this and feel even more confused about the poetic line now.

11. The cultural significance of Rayanne Graff is even more pertinent in 2016.

12. I remain firmly on the side of prose poetry, even though it remains a form that has fallen out of of style. It is hard to do well. I appreciate when it is done well. I think there are moments when I achieved it herein.

13. Confidence!

Zoe Whittall, 2016

CONTENTS

PART I: LINDA LOVELACE DIED TODAY

*I don't believe most
kids when they say they like the
Velvet Underground*

TREADING THE WORD

You have water, and the word water. You have love and the word love, but the two will never meet. We will lie beneath the letters in a haze of diaphanous pollution and probability, weighing our odds. *I love you* at the end of a phone call, it hovers, before the click signalling the end of the sentence, then it falls like equivocal truth. We are mostly water. We are mostly love. We are trying to quit smoking and sugar. We are ridding the body of the word Body. We hold red fruit between our teeth. Our gum-lines pink softened typewriter ribbon. We wrap our meat signing corporate jingles. You have no dental insurance and the words 'no dental insurance', and you carry *orajel* in your purse to stave off crying jags of frustration. You are my heart, and *you are my heart* stitched into a canvas. I hold thirty coffee beans. I count caloric value. You have water, the word water, and the body is mostly. We hold ours close. We say the words in hopes they are doing their job and not being as indeterminate as they are. Language tries its best. Language gets straight Cs. You have *kool-aid* and the word *kool-aid*, and the jingle comes when I'm sleeping. The taste is red. We drink water. We drink the word water. We lie beneath the W. We tell each other, *you are not filled with lack*. We sing beneath the R, treading the word.

6

SERENADE FROM THE PORCH AT THE PARKDALE GEM

1. I had a wisdom tooth pulled by a macho dentist at King and Dufferin whose nitrous machine didn't work. Through the window I watched a woman in cut-off sweat shorts throw her red pumps at a guy in plaid pants while the dentist sewed up my 3 stitches.

He called me tough.

My lover kept the tooth in a small tube meant for cocaine in a necklace around her neck. I mistook her action for devotion when it was simply accessorizing.

2. The first day of a bruise.

A June bug is making out with the porch light again. 40 watts vs. Scarab beetle.

Repeat : a giant ladybug with vertigo.

Rhonda's chihuahua barks at the ceramic bunny formed with willing hands to smile constantly. Leader of all porch ornaments, staring down the tiny shrubs, candy wrappers, water-logged paperbacks from the library at the end of the street. In the park the swing pines for WD-40.
I feel defeated pinching the bruise around its edge; my thumb and fingernail are making skinny hearts. Starving is not holy.

3. I'm nervous. Expecting sutures instead of flat skin
I'm waiting.
My eyebrows are giving me panic attacks.

4. Toronto Welcomes the Pope. Suddenly even the guy who
punches people outside the 7-11 is a believer.

Pilgrims are selling memorabilia on my way to work at the cafe
on Roncesvalles. Uniform red shoulder bags walking in packs,
singing hymns. Their eyes announce We Are Coming to Get You.
I drink too much coffee. It's free. I blend it with Fair Trade sugar
and cinnamon.

2 giant blue cups of water for the pregnant woman at table 2.

The cops sweep up undesirables—
please step back and allow the visitors to enjoy
the unobstructed view.

I sweep up the cafe floor.

At 3am on Church street, red-shouldered boys with Jesus T-shirts
kiss each other on the steps outside the Second Cup.

Later they yell *fucking dykes* when we walk to Blockbuster to rent
Ma Vie En Rose for the fourth time.

5. I almost died in a freight elevator on my way to get laid
by someone twice my age I couldn't even really talk to.

I chewed my nails until they bled, watered down prayers when
the box went black and the cables paused. Ridiculous faith when
fingers crossed. I wish I may, I wish I might.

The click and whirr sound of being saved
by invention.

6. Today I kicked the bank machine
other peoples' receipts stuck to my boot.

JUDY THIRTEEN

1. Judy will not wear this sweater again, the flawless one with the three-quarter length grey sleeves and black torso. Perfect thumbholes are worn-in around the wrists. Familiar. She wore it today and began choking on the bus, ready to die.

She coughed up the hard, red candy, expelling it onto graffiti written on the silver back of the bus seat. It said: "Save yourself first" and "I Love You."

Now the sweater is bad luck. She tossed it on top of the kitchen garbage before she brought it out the next morning. Her husband didn't notice.

2. She passed the funeral parlor on Marlon Road, the one between her house and her job at Stedman's department store. The undertaker outside was smoking, looked at her longer than he should, as if to say, "You're next, baby."

He watched her ass as she sashayed quickly back home to call in sick. Bad Luck. Judy rolls pennies on the plastic gingham tablecloth.

3. In the support group, there is a guy who chewed his own skin. There is a girl who fell a lot. There was a woman that Judy knew, just knew, wasn't going to make it. The therapist told Judy she was making progress, even though she had never spoken, just smiled.

4. When Judy got home she checked the pilot light again. Again. Again. Again. Again. She noticed a hole in her left sock.

5. Obsessed, prepossessed, infatuated, fixated, besotted, gripped, held, monomaniacal.
A visionary.

6. Her husband never ever worried. About anything. Sometimes when he was broke he would sigh a little bit. "Nothing to get all tense about, Jude," he said as he washed the carrots and set them aside. He rubbed a long one against the square metal grater. She knew wasn't worried about death. Disease. The possibility of both. Just the shreds of orange falling into the ceramic bowl. Sometimes this fact made Judy dream about chewing wine glasses.

7. Judy played harmonica in the window. The lady downstairs in the yard looked up. Her eyes were penny whistles.

8. Judy said "heaven forbid" whenever she thought about having sex with everyone on the bus. The old man, girl with braces. She couldn't stop it. She said "heaven forbid" without thinking she was saying it. It just came.

9. Fatalistic, skeptical, negative, dubious, abrogating, neutralizing, pessimistic.

10. The doctor said: "People with your condition either kill themselves or go on medication."

She took the script into the candy store. She bought red licorice and felt lighter.

11. Judy's mother telephoned every Monday night after bingo.
"How are you, sweetheart?"
"Nothing to complain about, you know, same old."

12. Last night when they fucked, she wanted to punch him in the head. She came, thinking he looked like a cowboy from the old western she watched the night before, when she couldn't fall asleep.

13. Judy remembered when God was a petal pulled in want. A first, second, third chew. A tangible fish. When it was God [.] Not God [?]

HER EYELASHES WERE LONG PERFECT WINGS CARRYING THE WEIGHT OF HER EYES

1. I read a poem about tranquilizers and love. I conjure my old roommate, Jane, whom I loved for 38 days. She had a mouth like a test tube.

She used to carry around enough pills to kill herself, in case the mood struck en route. But everyone went to her for advice. She told me the solution to my anxiety was to have a little more wine with dinner.

2. I would steal her copy of the Diagnostic and Statistical Manual of Mental Disorders IV and read it under the covers; waking early to put it back on the shelf between the bible and Pat Califia.

3. In the loft's bathroom with walls that don't meet the ceiling, I would splash cold water on my pallid face and look into the round mirror
a sublingual daydream.

4. The two stages of grief are

1) sadness
2) drinking

5. She looked across the table at me once and said, "If you keep staring at me like that, I'm going to come." I realized that after her hot, low voice, Jane's next attractive quality was her sociopathic potential. How often are you able to get that close to the apple? I left Jane's apartment quickly with my belongings in orange coloured milk crates. Her eyes were pinhole perfect watching me. She was dangerous like a slow grind on a last-call dance floor. Swivelled hips in circle eights.

22-year-olds
who own Toronto houses
kill my sense of calm

I LAUNDER, YOU LAUNDER, WE LAUNDER

1. In the basement laundry room of 137 Isabella Avenue, I can really see inside my mouth. A realist painting. Stark divergent shades of pinks. Teeth like square game pieces, tongue rolling the dice. Gaping open-hawed into the mirror.

2. The punch of a remaining metal filling last molar on the right side: in the copper alloy and mercury swirls a Saturday morning at the edge of seventeen and still drunk. My other dragged me to the dentist in the suburban mall that sat beside the ripped hemline of highway 20 outside of Montreal. I had to get cavities filled in before the insurance ran out. She sat in the waiting room reading Chatelaine while I tried to stop the bright lights from spinning, the fingers from gagging. I had an excellent gag reflex back then. My grade nine report card read, "She only does well in the subjects she enjoys." This crossed over to the school yard, the smoke pit, the yellow slides in the park.

3. Tiny islands of stored memory. The front one slightly chipped from a beer bottle and a gregarious hug hello. A stubborn baby tooth.

4. The laundry room is an x-ray machine. My blue hair leaves impressions everywhere. Little dots of indigo under my nails. Fine dark dust around my lips. When I lean against the wall, a shadow of my hair remains in the mirror a second longer than my mouth.

5. So forceful in that light. Clamped around my hand. Blistered knuckles. Bite sized moons.

6. I remember when Angela explained money laundering to me. We worked at a bar that was always renovating.

"It's how they launder money, duh." She always looked at me like I was a bright-eyed plush kitten from the toy section at an airport souvenir shop. Soft and empty. But she felt compelled to pick me up anyway, keep me solid on the dashboard of her truck.

7. I fold Q's white undershirts and remain fixated on my uvula. Not enough air in this room. My mouth a receptacle for bright light. Embrace, taste, fighting for my attention.

LINDA LOVELACE DIED TODAY

I wake up dizzy. Dry mouth in a full bathtub.

The dryer catches fire and fills the house with smoke. Once the windows are open, the sparks smothered, the cat digs her nail under mine.

Swell with me.

Linda Lovelace died today.

Kate calls: "I didn't ask you to be in my porn because you have a real career now, not because you're fat."

"Huh? My dryer is on fire. I have to go."

Sheets stained, hot knots of oxygen.

I call Kate back. "Linda Lovelace made *Deep Throat* at gunpoint. I overheard someone saying that on the bus and they were laughing."

I open each window, phone cradled in my soft neck, palms against wooden ledge painted over so many times it feels like I'm leaning on a pile of phonebooks, breathing in air instead of gagging on the smoke.

There is a man outside picking up bottles. He is singing Loretta Lynn. I expect him to spit but instead he stares.

Celexa was such
a smooth operator now
I feel every bone

TWO POEMS FOR EASTER MORNING

1.

We are looking for God. I pour tulips down the drain. We go to a Roncesvalles church on Easter morning. The church congratulates itself. We feel welcome and at odds. We just turned 30 and remembered about God. The minister, a bottle blond, reads a sermon: "CSI: Jerusalem." I whisper to you, "Does this make you believe in God any more than you don't?" You whisper, "I'm hungry so I'll take communion. Later, bagels." In our twenties we only thought about God when people killed themselves.

I come home to download American TV. A. sings along with *The Organ*. You go home. I wonder if you are lying to me again. I google obituaries. The pink daisy thrives. A. paints and paints with aplomb. Our house is filled with flowers and the freshest indie rock. We smoke on the from stoop like we live in an 80s sitcom set in Brooklyn. We try to make room for God. We forget to set a place for Jesus. But we don't have a kitchen table, so it's okay. Leave a sliver of couch where we could squeeze his holiness in between the cat scratches and the pile up of discarded bill envelopes. We all lie. We all, in the best 40 second intervals, tell the harshest truths through the colour bars of saline liquid. Every day our fingers yellow. Our eyes crease in the sun of the back balcony. The corner store is robbed. The cop says, "Please go back to your houses." I like to wake you up at dawn to ask you probing questions. Our verbs are mostly lazy on religious holidays. We take a cab on Dundas through church traffic while you lie or don't lie to me. You only leave when I ask. You won't leave. Me. I sit on the stoop waiting for you. Legs in the sun, ankles like apostrophes.

2.

I washed ashore, laid out on this pillow. My thoughts are night-shades. My wrists list ingredients. A. paints and paints. Warm and aging, like us. It was only a matter of time before I have up on the body. Yours and mine. It is one sight at a time. Your feet hurt in the morning and you call it "My stigmata! My stigmata feet hurt again!" I close my eyes on the Don Valley Parkway, certain of a collision. You think I'm holding out. Open your mouth and maybe. Look away and maybe.

PART II: OF SUB-CORTICAL BOTTLENECKS

PINK SHEETS

Vancouver is a city where pedestrians make loud sounds with their rain gear, where everything is enormous; the wind is a standing ovation, the mountains are a steady circle of salve, the ocean: an opening vein.

Watching traffic on Broadway street from Michael V.'s window I feel my chapped lips purse in the way she likes to draw them, curled in a smirk.

I turn on his pink sheets to where her head should be.

Back in Toronto, I leave eyeliner sketches on her clean pillows— potato prints on yellowed foolscap paper or two bruised eyes.

And I steal her expensive artist pens to write other girls' phone numbers on my arm in brackets while adamantly expressing my dislike for problematic terms like the *other girl*. I leave rings from my water glasses on the covers of her comic books and unpaid phone bills. I trample madly on soft, aching shoulders leave the vaguest trails of where I've been, I leave peanut butter on knives on the kitchen counter well past midnight while buzzing around with a spelling bee in my head.

In Vancouver, Michael V.'s pink cotton sheets around my missing body, my pink tongue dunks like a cookie into blueberry tea.

Later, at the writers' festival I think I hear an ecologist say "I'm an apologist."

And I don't feel I ever said sorry for making her leave that party while I stayed to run my hands up his leg kiss against the ground on Maitland street arrive home drunk at dawn citing a smothered heart, an almost-30 crisis for juvenility and the joy excess brings.

Watching Vancouver from a sixth floor Broadway window I want her.

DIRT ROAD WEDDING

In Vancouver for a family wedding
I am foot sore lost
in the bridal shop,
lungs heavy.

Everyone asks me,
"Where's your boyfriend?"
and I say,
"In 1989."

THE PHARMACEUTICAL GENERATION

Makes me feel like a bad fad,
a trucker cap from the Gap.

My mouth is knit with synthetic yarn.
My hands are pools of cocoa butter lotion.

I stop taking pills and when I turn corners
I wake up in a sweat.

It's irrational.
(Oh, then I understand.)

It's easier to think of it like science.
Science explains stupidity.

Science is a warm hug
by a sweatered father.

When you're crazy, and you find someone else
who is also crazy, it's like you cancel each other out.

BLACK OUT 2006/03

It's a black out. When it's dark, and we are in vague despair, we look for the light at the end of her cigarette to direct us towards the door. Inside I count to ten every time she says something for the fiftieth time. We take the stairs. There is no elevator. I talk about how drunk I am because I am not an alcoholic. When I do drugs, I tell everyone I'm on drugs. Tell-tale truths, unusual comforts, peppermint cuts on my tongue, the lights were always on. It is a flicker. The city keeps going. We keep swallowing. There is no black out.

HALL BUILDING PROSE MASSACRE

In a 1994 writing class I wrote a first-person story based on my life at the time. It was fast, flawed, inorganic and riddled with a cherubic innocence. The characters swore too much, wore an excess of eyeliner, believed in love and revolution, purity and possibility. 5 classmates, pencil nubs chewed, eyes narrowing, agreed that the main character was a sociopath. I cried all the way home, to prove that I wasn't.

by Nick Drake on the juke box at a bar called *the Communist's Daughter*. I run my hand on his back, lay it still like a floating minnow at the base of his spine. His muscled arms are taut and as I stroke them, feel each vein, we're talking each other up and down. Next track is Elliot Smith's *2:45 in the Morning* and we say the next song we choose won't be by someone who's killed themselves. Whatever this feeling is right now, it's not lasting, it's electric and moving so fast I'm surprised I can see it. Just electrons moving around, that's all. It can be explained in simple terms. It takes us to a kiss in an alley, a bank machine embrace, another pint, another late taxi, another loonie for three songs. He says I was nervous to meet you, I changed my shirt three times.

ELEVEN THOUGHTS ON THE DAY SHIFT

1. The girl in the park holds her cigarette like a thermometer—after she eats a Big Mac from her curled fist every day at two-fifteen. She's thin as a pipe-cleaner, a heart monitor line. She has a ponytail as clumsy as my animosity towards her. I eat my quinoa and broccoli, glaring through my box office window.

2. I am wearing a lot of red these days to make up for my pale lips, my walk-on part eyes, the shortened sunlight. A Canadian B-celebrity is in a play at the theatre and everyone is kissing his ass. I ask him for a ticket stub to his own show. I get a warning. The bartender sneaks me shots of whiskey in a coke can after intermission and we tell each other who is sleeping with who, which in a gay theatre, is an intricate tree of hands and mouths.

3. It takes 40 cups of coffee to kill you. I want to test this theory but my girlfriend, sipping blueberry tea slowly says *your impulsivity is unsettling*. She brings me a double Americano and a straw when the plays last more than two hours.

4. My nipples refuse to be contained today. Full moon provides no bidning power. A man on the streetcar reeaches for the right one to pull like a pinball lever. I muster a truncated series of stuttered swears and spit next to his unbuckled boot.

5. Our apartment is a rough draft. Pencil lines. Scratch marks. Perfect paragraphs. Is this common-law? See shelving unit purchased together. Now that marriage is legal, I'm thinking of going out for a pack of cigarettes like men do in the movies.

6. I was given a free banana from the mean waiter where everyone at the theatre orders take-out. "Here, take!" he said gruffly. I placed it neatly by the cash register and stared at it all day, waiting, like it was a future batch of good ideas.

The accountant asks me "Do you have any food?" and I slide the banana under the ticket booth window. He thanks me as if I'd rescued him from a natural disaster.

Later, I wonder if I could have used the potassium.

7. The accountant, whose name is also a verb, announces "I have a moral quandry!" over the intercom. Coworkers make fun of my too-professional sounding page voice, leftover from my last job as a corporate secretary.

For example: "Accounts recievable, line one."
A stage tech responds with, "I feel like a bumblebee."
He gives swooning eyes to the dimpled-girl stage manager, who pretends she doesn't notice.

8. There is a man who looks like Willie Nelson, without the music, sitting in the park. My coworker hates him because he is homeless and needing cigarettes. I am indifferent to Willie Nelson until he looks at me hard, like you would a cherry pie behind a plastic layered-twirl tray at a roadside diner. Now I hate him too.

9. Yesterday it was my yellow cardigan, mis-buttoned, in the reflection of the porn store window. Today it's the way my boss writes everything with improper quotation marks. The sign reads: "FIVE" pointers for "Excellent" customer service!

10. I doodle "Go Ask Alice Munro" on the back of a ticket stub while trying to look busy. I decide it will be the new title of my book of un-sellable short stories. Publishers always say two things about short fiction collections: "Short stories aren't marketable." And "You should read Alice Munro to know how it's done." My boss tells me to stop doodling on tickets, stop taking imaginary smoke breaks because it makes me look like I'm not doing anything.

11. Zoloft makes me completely fine. I have never felt so fine about feeling nothing. Nothing makes me feel complete. I live about my neck. My head is an orchid in full bloom. When I am fake nice, I am actually nice. "No, really, have a nice day!" I sing from behind the plastic window of the box office. My coworker announced she is afraid of botulism and won't eat anything from a can. It makes me want to buy her flowers.

LOVE IS NOT AN ACCEPTABLE TITLE FOR ANYTHING

I hate it when people put their bus transfers in their mouths for no reason, take off their socks and shoes on a slushy cold bus. I hate it when doctors mix you up with other patients. What part of my isn't a fucking STAR? I hate it when people use anatomically correct words for body parts during sex. Once, he said the V word, and I had to get up, leave, and never return to his bed nestled above the regent park beer store. I even left my favourite pair of underwear under his sheets and decided they were a sacrifice.

*GM sells more
porn
than Larry Flynt*

FROM THE GLADSTONE HOTEL

She says that she considered suicide the same
way she considered taking a shower

I flirt so badly now that
I think too much

I made out with my favourite fag for a photo op
(you looking for company? ... we are the company!)

The girl in the band looks so much like
my first girlfriend that I threw up a little

Everyone at breakfast got drunk
last night at a goth wedding

On Dufferin street even
the sunlight is dirty

They break up over her
relationship status on Friendster

Jealousy is amusing
six months later

A girl I know runs the lesbian history
archives—I save things in a file for her

Writers make bad housewives
but excellent stalkers

FRONT OF HOUSE

I want to write a poem for the cheap glitter face makeup frozen to my eyelashes making me see another dimension to his flat one-syllable complexion, winter aloof eyes. I carry want like shards of bottle glass in my pockets weighing down my walk away. Bar to the box office. Shrug of the mop water.

I can always spot
the one real lesbian in
girl on girl porn films

827 OSSINGTON

A choke-cherry red holler erupts from the tree turn growing inside my right lung. My hard, mean palms serenade the ice as I fall. In Toronto snow is the colour of emphysema against a snail hue sky.

I have only cried once since I kissed her goodbye. It was a sign, I remember thinking, that every meal I made her turned out awful. The steak at our last dinner shunned by ravenous housecats.

I always end relationships on Ossington street. It's long and grey, bookended by the mental hospital and a gas station that got bombed last week.

SATISFYING SOFT VICTORIES

1) Pushing 7 to erase a message that doesn't matter anymore

2) Remembering and using long division

3) Figuring out something seemingly simple about a society bent on beauty. Sitting at work, trying not to eat anything but carrots. Think about how stalling ingestion can be a triumph of will. Is thin simply sexier or a symptom of moral worth?
Wonder if: a sharp edged soft-pink packet of Sugartwin, a day of just saliva and strength = pure achievement?

4) A very small dog in a big park

CARTOGRAPHY OF AN ANXIOUS GIRL

Am I going to fall off this metal bar? My centre of gravity is in my pelvis. His, in his shoulders. I watch Jimmy climb to the top of the monkey bars. I am halfway up. Because I am small, this measure of height causes my heart to pound. What keeps Jimmy from jumping off the highest rung? After all, where else could he go? Will he simply be happy, just sitting at the top, the winner?

Will he not be crestfallen?

He smiles, stupidly. I am jealous of how stupid Jimmy is. I am jealous when people are not crazy. I do not realize this is what I'm feeling. In that time, against the metal bar, sweaty in my palms, I feel an ache. Wrinkling beside my ten year old eyes.

When I see the ocean for the first time, I don't care. I want to go back to the car where it was circular, and I was dreaming about sex. I don't know about sex yet. Or I don't know in words, just imaginings. I was a warm feeling. There was only a picture in my brain. Of two people tied to a metal hanging structure. The ocean was a side bar. I was both of them. I was told not to look or feel. I was melting chemicals and I was warmer than I'd ever been.

I kneeled in the sand while the others walked to the picnic baskets. Reaching my hand down in, I scooped up and tasted the grit and salt.

Who cares? Is this what the fuss is about?

I am a morbid child. Christmas, the ocean, and the first snowfall escape me.

Sunsets are sometimes not so bad.

These are the times I love. When I want so much that the wanting is the whole point. I could die ecstatic in my expecting. I watch the cutest boy across the street, sitting the park with his guitar. I never want to meet him. The eventual pain of getting, arriving, is not the point.

My mouth is dry. My hands are full of lotion.

I stop taking pills and when I turn corners, I keep swirling in circles. I am a human tilt-a-whirl.

I'M 16, DRIVING HOME FROM BALTIMORE

1. He always stands to the right of my door after ringing the bell so I can't see who's standing on my porch. I want to see what he looks like when he's anticipating. I run down my stairs and trip, fall forward, knees to dirty carpet, all because I can't stop rolling my eyes. Why must he make everything so monumentally clandestine?

2. Everyone looks good in unconventional green coats.

3. I cut fruit in circles and squares on the phone with Lisa, steam kale and admit I'm giving up on the poetry tour, not handing in my grant, going back to work at the bar. I'm not jumping anymore without a safety net. I shuffle the cards. I turn 29 and sweep the floor.

4. I can't stop thinking about the only thing I remember him saying the other night
"You are the one I let get away." We talked for hours and I don't remember anything but the bourbon. I vaguely remember punching him in the arm as a response.

5. Two drinks only.

6. resolve
sprinkle with lemon juice
unearth
deny
repeat

7. My rough drafts are always covered in eyeliner fingerprints.

8. I got off the bus at Yonge street, my least favourite part of the
rotten core. My legs feel heavy, a wormhole heart. I feel drugged,
my heart races, then a flash: OH, THIS. I REMEMBER THIS. I
can fuckin' beat this. Red face.
Racing thoughts: zero.
Me: ten points.

9. Someone is always the sucker. It won't always be me.

Clasp your hands. She is not a precious stone. Remember you did not like holding hands because of the height difference. Buy ripe fruit with few bruises. Hum a sad song quickly. Bathe in vinegar. Lather in shea butter. Buy a new pen. When people ask you on dates, say yes, don't pretend you can't hear them. If you miss her, it only means you miss her. Remember that you won't ever remember it right. Remember that you knew, long before you really knew, that it wasn't meant to last. Spend your last ten dollars. Take-Out. Hair dye. Remember that you learned the definitions of "need" and "want" in grade 9 economics class from the teacher who was always drunk. Watch *CSI Miami* and cheer on Horatio. *Go Horatio, you can love again, Horatio*. Nobody is thinking of you right now. Nobody is thinking of her, except you. Point your toes when you sit on the bus and your feet won't touch the ground. Buy ingredients and put them together. Bathe in lavender. Disengage. Remember that you don't remember. Hold your own hand.

PART III: SCRAPS AGAINST THE SCREEN

June 6th. 1985
Dear Judy Blume,

I'd just like to start by saying that I am the biggest fan of yours that ever was. I started with *Superfudge* in Grade 2 and have read everything you've ever written, with the exception of a certain very important chapter in FOREVER which the school library has cut out. Can you please send me that chapter, you know, the one where they do it? I think it's only fair, as I am your biggest fan, and should get some perks.

Forever yours,
Zoe

Dear Boy George,

When I told my mother I was going to marry you as soon as I was old enough to take the bus to Montreal by myself and go see you are your concert, she said that probably would never happen. And it didn't. Please explain.

My love forever,
Zoe

June 1, 1989
Dear Axl Rose,

I'm writing to clarify a few things. First of all I know you party a lot and everything but I need you to remember your last concert at Montreal's Olympic Stadium. My friend Janey, skinny, blond, a-cups, anyway, she said that you sang the song "Patience" looking right at her the whole time. She also said that after the show, she gave you and the blond drummer guy blowjobs. I need to know if this is true or not because Janey became really popular since that show and I need some confirmation. She's really annoying me.

Love,
Zoe

p.s. She was only 13 so if you don't answer me I'm going straight to Circus magazine about this.

Dear Rayanne Graff,

Did you ever stop to think that maybe Angela was your one true love, your Jordan Catilano, right under your pretty pierced nose? It showed in the episode where you got drunk and traded shoes in the parking lot of a bar.
Purposeful subtext or not, it showed.
We were watching you.

Love,
Zoe

September 1991
Dear Emily Valentine,

You were such a welcome break from the Betty/Veronica tedium of Brenda and Kelly. The monotonous creeping virus that was Donna's virginity. Let's not even begin to discuss the receding hairlines of high school boys. Let's focus on lack of things to do most Wednesday nights in suburban Montreal except long for the ocean-strewn hair and boyfriends with a car. Oh Emily, your hair was enough to cause problems. You existed to turn the boys on before you turned to violence. You green-eyed every girl with your insistence on madness and interrupted femininity. You couldn't really exist for longer than a hot flash, Emily, cause when you rode up to West Beverly on your motorcycle, you were a futuristic bad-girl, who couldn't blend into the Happy Days of California dreaming. You lit cars on fire before you were locked up. And you had to be locked up. I was hoping for a spin-off, Miss Valentine. What happened?

Love,
Zoe

Dear Molly Ringwald,

You were once a heroine to the girls from the wrong side of the tracks with your slapdash perfect prom dresses and Psychedelic Furs soundtrack. Recently I went on a date with a twenty-one-year-old boy who didn't know who you were. This made me feel old.

Fuck you, Molly Ringwald.

Love,
Zoe

Dear Corey Haim,

As the years go by, I'm less and less able to differentiate between you and Mr. Feldman, even though for half a decade, I slept beneath your shiny teen-beat faces proclaiming each different Corey trait by heart. Do you miss the spotlight, the rumours linking you and Miss Gibson? Do you feel as loved as you did in the 80s? Is fame a parasitic, crippling disease or is that just something un-famous people say to make themselves feel okay about their anonymity?

Love,
Zoe

LAW AND ORDER: AN EROTIC PRIMER

It begins with Jill Hennessey,
as Assistant District Attorney, Claire Kincaid

in the early years, (when aids and reverse racism
were de riguer)
her Grace-Jones intonation +
the perfect,
single cocked brow =
                    hungry for righteousness,
acclaim
a sensible brown suit, the front steps of the court-house

                                In the criminal justice system

we were rapt while
she pined for

                                D.A. McCoy,

who could tie a cherry stem around a jury's tongue,
the way he spoke *docket, evidence, objection!*

We spoke back: *dockut, evuhdince, objectshun!*

He knew who to kill for the killing
              and after, with a solid nod towards justice
              stroll straight into the smoke-soaked cop bar
resigned, thoughtful, virile

god-like, Mr. Wolf, god-like

In the age of the Special Victims Unit,

Oh, Olivia

there is a masterful masculinity,
a minty-breathed manipulation
the spine-straight episodic triumphs over misogyny
       he melts through pixels, the detective
       with the muscles and the bad marriage

                his anger managed fitfully
                the way his fist lands on the
           side of good

    always

                the way he serves and protects

she was a single mother
(twist!)
a sociopath!

say it slow

                the people are represented by two

equally

Law & Order, it was you first

Oh, Claire

Before I gleaned any fundamental forensic tan-lined
quasi knowledge from *CSI Miami*

(*Oh, Horatio, take those shades off slowly
say it slower, like you're reading a flashcard
in a 70s porno
I think, it was his time, to diiiiiie.*)

I cut my teeth on Claire and Jack
            my moral code, sculpted
at 7pm in sundication.
            Watch them, on Omni 1. Take note.

In bed, say to your lover:

*Tell me what to do now, Jack.
Say it slower, harder, harder, more!*

Yeah.

These are their stories.

PART IV: DENIAL CHASERS

ON DISCOVERING

1. On re-discovering my love of pot :

Did I just ! brush my teeth ! for an hour?
I remember this feeling from recess!

2. On discovering how to love myself again :

my red bra falls out of my purse and onto the counter at the
Portuguese bakery where I buy my coffee on the mornings after.
The bakery is between our houses exactly. The woman with the
stubby band-aid makes me a latte without flinching.

3. On re-discovering self-esteem on January 2 :

Having .23 in my chequing
.47 in my savings
and a two day old coke hangover
is no reason to feel as bad about myself
as I do right now

ARISE, KING OF TERABITHIA

It's me plus the colour bars again; a dreamy and sombre duet.
I wish insomnia made me productive: dirty bath-tub, dying celery
in the crisper, half-finished art projects on the floor.

Instead, I have perfected the vaguely pointed stare,
psychological eye games with my cat,
the filing and re-filing of the perfect long nail.

I read emails from my dyslexic cousin who works as a ship-hand
in Florida. They are hard to decipher but make me love him.
When he came to visit our farm in the early 80s, my mother
said "Robert doesn't drink." and for years I thought that he had
superhuman powers, not needing any water to stay alive.

DENIAL CHASERS

Under these circumstances
I'd like to pretend
the drinks you pour me
are
apostrophes
housed in triples disguised as doubles
back against boxes of empties
surprising you by the pulse
of the industrial dishwasher

ACKNOWLEDGEMENTS

"Judy Thirteen" originally appeared in *Broken Pencil*. "Poem for the Other Side of the Apartment Door" originally appeared in *Kiss Machine*, Volume 11, and was re-printed in *Geist*. "Dear Molly Ringwald" and "Law & Order: An Erotic Primer" appeared in *Matrix*, early versions of "Linda Lovelace Died Today" and "Six Thoughts on a Parkdale Porch" appeared in *Breathing Fire 2: Canada's New Poets* edited by Patrick Lane and Lorna Crozier.

The fan letters were written for Trash and Ready, a trio of word-based performance artists co-founded with Hadassah Hill, Lisa Foad, and Tara-Michell Ziniuk. "Dear Boy George," "Dear Axl Rose," and "Dear Judy Blume" appeared on our CD *Bombshell Lexicon* produced by Thomas Sinclair. Lyrics from Kids on TV appear in *from the Gladstone Hotel* with permission.

ABOUT THE AUTHOR

Zoe Whittall is the author of four novels, most recently *The Best Kind of People* (House of Anansi, 2016) and *Holding Still for as Long as Possible* (Anansi, 2010). She published her third collection of poetry, *Precordial Thump*, in 2008 with Exile Editions. She works as a TV writer and novelist in Toronto.

INVISIBLE PUBLISHING is a not-for-profit publishing company that produces contemporary works of fiction, creative non-fiction, and poetry. We're small in scale, but we take our work, and our mission, seriously: We publish material that's engaging, literary, current, and uniquely Canadian.

We are committed to publishing diverse voices and experiences. In acknowledging historical and systemic barriers, and the limits of our existing catalogue, we strongly encourage writers of colour to submit their work.

Invisible Publishing continues to produce high-quality literary works, and we're also home to the Bibliophonic series, Snare, and Throwback imprints.

If you'd like to know more please get in touch:
info@invisiblepublishing.com

Invisible Publishing
Halifax & Picton